CATACLYSMIC VIBRATIONS

CATACLYSMIC VIBRATIONS

© Stuart Watkins 2022

All rights reserved

Stuart Watkins hereby asserts his moral right
to be known as the author of this work.

This book is sold subject to the conditions that it shall not, by way of trade or otherwise, be lent, re-sold, hired out or otherwise circulated without Stuart Watkins' prior consent, in any form of binding or cover other than that which it is published, and without a similar condition including this condition being imposed on the subsequent purchaser.

ISBN: 9798356820151

Cataclysmic Vibrations

Stuart Watkins

Table of Contents

Prologue 6
Gemini and Capricorn 11
Alliterative Biopsy (Allibi) 14
Psychotic Episode 15
Amoeba 17
St. Boris 19
Hecate's Fate 22
Curse of the Inquisitor 24
Ocean's End 29
Albatross 33
A Game of Chess 36
BBC (Britain and BrylCreem) 42
The Wrath of Mars 48
Sapio-Crush 50
The Philosopher 53
Assertion of Self 58
I Determine 63
Anxiety and Depression 65
The Weirdness of it 68
The Black Death? 77
Trickle 82

A COVID Ode	84
Dust and Ashes	86
Year of the Dragon	89
The Eyes of Azrael	94
Fourteenth Frequency Riddle	96
One	101
Glasshouses and Stones	103
Methuselah and Sphinx	106
The Visibility of the Toxicity	108
Cataclysmic Vibrations	111

Prologue

I wrote my first poem at the age of eight, as an assignment that our teacher had set for us in English. The only theme we were issued with, was that it had to be about an animal. After a few seconds' deliberation I settled for a cobra. In general, quick decisions, that I then stick with, have served me very well. Plus, as I will come back to, a little darkness usually surfaces when I think.

The resulting piece was entitled 'Cobra, Cobra', and it had four verses that each had 'Cobra, Cobra' as the first line. I don't recall anything more about the actual wording, but of course we all remember how things make us feel in life, and so when the poem was publicly praised as the best one written, and then posted on the school notice board, the only one that was, it was a memorable event.

Unfortunately, I did not keep a copy, and so it vanished from the face of the earth.

What did remain though, was the reinforcement of my innate confidence, that I was able to write and create out of nowhere. In years to come my path was to deviate away from 'Right Brain' artistic and creative neural pathways, in favour of 'Left Brain' analytical and logical ones, so I studied sciences at school and university instead. It was a long time later in life that I found my way back from Left to Right. Nowadays I have a decent amalgamation of the two.

Over the years, I would occasionally put pen to paper (literally, some of the time), or tippy-tap on the keys of typewriters, and later word processors, because something within me decided there was a creation wanting to reveal itself. As many writers will testify, often a poem or passage will appear to write itself.

Poetry became an occasional result of those moments.

In my twenties I accumulated a number of poems. Typically, I would write them and then leave them alone for periods of time and then dig them out for re-reads, and the re-reads might result in the destruction of the pieces altogether, or they'd be retained after being approved of.

Some interesting work was lost.

Then, in 2019, despite my positive opinions about my poems, I was motivated again by internal rather than external forces - to write a 'Left Brain' book. The issue of Brexit was the catalyst to the beginning of the project, but very soon I decided to also comment on other serious matters. I also decided that to just sit and write continuous prose was too predictable as it is the method of construction of most books, and so I experimented with style and format, in particular 'loose prose', a lazy technique I devised that enables a writer to say more, but with less words.

I had just found access to the Amazon 'Kindle Direct Publishing' platform too, meaning I was able to not just write, but also proof-read, edit, and format all the text, but to also design the artwork.

Therefore, no agent or publisher, that might presume to 'muscle in' on the content, style or royalties.

The subjects I chose to analyse, in **'A United Kingdom' - Trains of Logical Thought**, using the critical thinking skills that my science background had helped me to develop since school and university, were;

Abortion
Religion
Brexit
The Subconscious Mind (I have suffered with schizophrenia for 28 years, so my mind is strange)
The Monarchy (and whether it is actually the 'good value for money' we are often told)
The paths of privilege (via Eton and Oxford)
The NHS
Pornography (and the ominous social timebomb of free teenage access to it)
The tobacco industry
Television
Propaganda
Advertising
The individual styles of Tony Blair, David Cameron, Theresa May and Margaret Thatcher.

Some people have kindly suggested that the book should be studied at sixth form or university. Others are of the opinion that it should be banned. Either way, I am proud of the contents.

Having 'popped my cherry' as a published writer, I wanted to resurrect any poems that I still felt deserved to be 'out there'. I proceeded to vet my work, was inspired to write more pieces, and reached a stage where I thought there were enough to construct a collection for publication. Much of the poetry was abstract in nature, veering into the metaphysical, and I used as a title the one which I had been keeping under wraps for years. **Cosmic Visions** was published in 2021. As well as the weirder pieces there are love poems and some silly comedy. I reached out to musicians and there were collaborations that arose; the Ukrainian multi-instrumentalist, Antony Kalugin, used my poem 'Key' and extracts from 'Tower of Stone', while the Dutch rock band Lesoir used the philosophical 'Ephemeral' at the climax of their epic 20-minute song 'Babel', that has an accompanying masterpiece of CGI animation by Crystal Spotlight.

My mother died in the summer of 2019, on the 20th June, but due to those infamous COVID-19 lockdowns, that were treated as optional by certain unscrupulous politicians, we were not able to scatter her ashes at sea, and they stayed at my father's home until the summer of 2021. On the second anniversary of her passing, a blisteringly hot day, we were able to say goodbye to her, and for a few reasons it motivated me to write a short book about it - and so **The Ocean** came into being. As usual I used original ingredients - including photographs taken at Walmer beach on the day, and a zodiacal, elemental poem of violent anguish.

During the pandemic, I wrote a poem entitled 'A COVID Ode' expressing a sarcastic viewpoint of the pandemic which then precipitated the creation of a Facebook Group which I simply called 'Pandemic Poets'. The group grew to 456 members - with some of them submitting pieces, which they had either already written or that were written specifically for the group. Both quality and quantity of submissions were sufficient to facilitate an anthology, and so the collection **Pandemic Poets** was born.

While working through the curation of Pandemic Poets I had other projects in progress. My many years of contributions to

Facebook, and to a much lesser extent, Twitter, have grown into a substantial book, in fact it was in progress prior to Pandemic Poets. Due to the momentum that was increasing, though, it made more sense to bring Pandemic Poets ahead of it.

The social media extracts project, with its lovely but secret title, is at an advanced stage. I keep my favourite social media comments, as I post them online, to this day, and so that book is expanding and evolving constantly. It will be published in 2023.

And that brings us to this book. I had a few newer poems and hit a purple patch where I was writing new material quite prolifically, and so it overtook everything else. The themes were darker than before. They had threads in common, broadly about disruptions in fields of energy, both physical and psychological. As these themes progressed it made sense for it to become a twin flame or sibling to Cosmic Visions, and **Cataclysmic Vibrations** came to be.

Stuart Watkins, October 2022.

Gemini and Capricorn
(a story of stormy love)

I don't exist outside of you.

I don't want to, even for the blink of an eye.
I'm certain I'd be ground with a pestle and mortar
into crumbs, into powder.

I'd surrendered my sovereignty, that very first day,
the anticipated rush,
the wave of the euphoric shiver,
the shudder, the tremor of tension.

Your arms are a cradle of Autumn warmth.
Our bed, a haven from the bite of Winter,
a cold and icy frost, a cocoon, a chrysalis,
protected, armoured.

Where did I go?

When was the momentary switch?
Was it creeping, was it slow,
was it undiscernable, impossible to know?
No focal beam, or turning lathe of form?
Silhouette, outline, visible shape or early warning?
The bliss and elation of our very first morning.

Perhaps my urgency and electricity forced the fateful path,
manifested in a magic of merging mind and matter.

CATACLYSMIC VIBRATIONS

I don't exist outside of you, and I don't want to.

Advance, this dance, by 10 insane years.
This fog of freedom and release
becomes a today from a yesterday.
I didn't notice the decadence of our decade,
our drama and our dream,
and our desperate devotion with its positive pain.

Every angstrom of distance apart
is an agonising harpoon to the heart,
though I'd still find a well
for the acid of my temper.

Your unbreakable, indestructible adoration
allows my comfort zone
to extend to psychobabbled anger,
when the kitchen bin is too full.

How dare you be that lazy.

Moments later, you find out
that I've forgotten to buy
the right brand of sparkling water, and
the shoe switches feet with a shock,
and I face the fire and fevered fury
of your Irish and Spanish ancestors.

I love you, and every last idiosyncrasy, so much.

Nobody should fear their life-amorous partner.
"Fear isn't useful anyway,
don't bother with it", I say,

aloofly, convincing myself I'm sounding like
Elon Musk, or Einstein.

We're not really scared, however loud the voices.
If you never shouted at me,
or stood your ground so beautifully,
when I bellow my pointless beefs,
the fizzle-out would have ruthlessly fired
the white-hot kiln of boredom
within two lunar cycles.

Silence and howling wolves are easy to choose between,
no ponderation required.
Placidity and soft-speak
are not for war-torn warriors like us.

Gemini and Capricorn,
astral twins,
make a formidable, Olympian team,
and though it was never said aloud,
the certainty was aflame in the furnace of our souls,
long before my excited, frantic stumble
on that Wiltshire road.

We just knew, everything.
Every single thing.

I don't exist without you,
and I don't want to.

Alliterative Biopsy (Allibi)

Prestigious, proud, professional projects
progressing presently,

weaving webs while wild, weeping willows
wane wistfully.

Poetry peeps past prose's perilous,
potentially paradoxical, portentous pathways.

Abstract, artistic angels amble and ache,
after apocalyptic, absolute, asphyxiative archways.

Psychotic Episode

I'm suddenly in a bubble of irrational fears;
they oscillate and tease between panic and tears.
A brand new terror, after 30-odd years,
announces its presence like poison-tipped spears.
Bobbing in a nightmare of dark orbs and spheres.

There's sweat on my brow and there's sweat in my bed;
a universe of horrors - all inside my head;
showers of scarlet and bloodstains of red,
claws tear my body, lacerate and shred;
the floor will consume me, where can I tread?

Every sound, every noise - it's coming for me.
Must I try to escape? Am I safe in a tree?
Will a locked door protect me, will the evil find me?
Can it feel every breath, intelligently?
Does it read all my thoughts and my desperate Chi?

I'm locked up in here, these surroundings are new,
Everything's foreign, their faces are blue.
They stare at my soul, I can't tell what is true.
Accusing and damning, and pointing "It's YOU".
I'm trying to run but my feet are in glue.

I know that their aim is to rip out my heart;
talons will scratch me and tear me apart.
I have no defence, there's nowhere to start,
this mob, they're angry, they each want a part
of my flesh, my bones and my science and art.

My dreams are reality, reality's a dream,
my voice doesn't carry; it's pointless to scream.
I can't make connections, there isn't a theme,
every thought scrambles and burns me in steam.
Unravelling sanity to the utmost extreme.

I'm told it's paranoia but it's definitely real.
Hours are minutes, the clock's like a wheel.
They push me their tablets, crushed in my meal.
Where is this dimension with its bars of steel?
They're keeping me safe……but that's not how I feel.

Amoeba

Nobody else knows what this is like;
to be this small and insignificant;
to be so over-awed by everything I see,
and everything I hear. I need help.

I am Tantalus, I lunge for nothing.
I am Damocles, I dread the sword.
I am Atlas, my back is breaking.
I am Sisyphus, destined never to rest.

I do not matter. I am the least of matter.
A single cell, in a wishing well.
All passes me by as I wait here to die.
A splodge on a splidge in a single raindrop.

It seems there are millions of me.
I'm damned though, if I can tell.
I see only translucency.
I see endless emptiness, and no emphasis.

I'm too microscopic to dream;
I know things are not as they seem;
The lowest of matter, *sans*-brain;
I loiter among the mundane.

My purposeless life is a waste,
I don't understand why I'm here;
no mind, Ikigai, nor belief;
no flight on the back of a leaf.

But one consolation I have;
you can always confuse a dumb chav;
no matter how tiny I am,
people follow me on Instagram.

St. Boris

We all know of St. Francis of Assisi.
A man born into privilege, that turned away
to follow, instead, a religious path.

In modern-day England, we are blessed with
the presence of
St. Boris of Fibonacci, also known as 'Fib'.

Dear Alexander Boris de Pfeffel,
did you win that job in a raffle?
Because everyone thinks you're a joke,
if they haven't been taking a toke.
Your Pinocchio nose spans the Thames.
It's longer than hollyhock stems.

One can hear the snickers in the House,
as if feeding a Snickers to a mouse,
politicians distrusting their ears,
zig-zagging from laughter to tears,
as the latest gaffes and black lies
mask the cheese, the wine and black ties.

Which wares are you pushing today?
A vaccine, policy or way?
A 'briefing', a plug of a drug,
or Rishi's new con? He looks smug.
You know that we know that you know

CATACLYSMIC VIBRATIONS

that we Brits reap the apathy we sow.
We know that you know that we know
that the Press are the Stop and the Go.
The B and the B and the C
call the shots, temporarily,
but the ebb and the flow of the tide
have turned, and there's nowhere to hide.

The Future's not Orange, it's Red.
We know that we're already dead.
The ill-gotten gains of corruption
are worthless among self-destruction,
whether nuclear war or the sun,
the race of humanity is run,

and our thin, foolish pride is for nowt.
Everyone's on the way out.
Famine, sunstroke and drought.
No scream, scared whimper or shout

will stop or divert the mad dogs,
in this plague of rabies and frogs.

It's certain we're beckoning doom,
we just don't know the shape of its room.
An annihilation and blast
that would fuse present, future and past,

One moment, one karma, one fate.
One love becoming one hate.

Mount Megiddo towers to the sky.
It silently watches us die.

CATACLYSMIC VIBRATIONS

Armageddon's crack or crescendo
was never just soft innuendo.
We're owners of all we survey
'neath the brittle shadow of today.

Hecate's Fate

The search for a mate.
To eliminate hate from our lives.
To cultivate a state of calm.
To accumulate a leg and an arm.
To locate our soulmate.
To formulate a strategy to thrive.
To appreciate, to educate, to survive.

To be accurate.
To be celibate.

To calculate the aggregate of our fate.
To reverberate, to oscillate, to participate.
To anticipate, to wait, to bear the weight.
To speculate on the state of the state.
Above all, to replicate and propagate.
Not to berate, hesitate or pontificate.
Follow the triumvirate.

To concentrate.
To estimate.
To meditate.
To spectate.

To decorate, to marinate.
To mutate, to mutilate.
To masticate, to masturbate.

To operate, animate, negotiate.
To complicate, dissipate, isolate.
To duplicate, understate, overstate.

The desolate and the intricate.
The nitrate and the sulphate.
The carbonate and the permanganate.
To correlate, ruminate and navigate.

To inflate.
To deflate.
To conjugate, coagulate.
To implicate, incriminate, incarcerate.
To instigate, imitate.
To frustrate, to tolerate.

Choose a candidate.
Shut the gate to your estate,
record the date,
clear your plate,
clean the slate,
count to eight,
be sure to respirate,
let it culminate,
and let it terminate.

Curse of the Inquisitor

For all of us, there are blessings that we can count.
For some of us, they are abundant,
for others they are sparse and few.
For some of us, perspective assists in the positives,
and for others, only the doubts and the negatives.
The morning sunshine is enough to radiate all day for some
even if the rain pours from midday to the twilight.
Yet if the day begins in soft drizzle,
there are those that cannot smile,
regardless of the improvement in the weather in the meanwhile.

Our temperament is governed by the stars, some will say.
Our zodiac sign dictating the mood, and rate of decay.
Whatever else ensues, I am at the mercy of the Earth
for the Goat was assigned as my keeper at my moment of birth.
We each have a limited amount of control
over what we are able to feel, or accomplish, at any point.
Yet random and impromptu events, influences,
will fly, or pass by, as we try to direct our nuances.

I know of people that believe they have total command
of every minute of their every day.
The paths that their lives follow, do often bear out
the veracity of their beliefs in this way.
Others will tell you that there are forces of destiny in play.
An omnipotent and omnipresent director
making every decision, for everybody,
whether it be pitch black, or snow white, or a muddy grey.

CATACLYSMIC VIBRATIONS

Then there is absence and abdication of order.
Madness. Mayhem.
Nothing can be affected, no person having any power.
All any of us can do is ride on the tide
of the wideness of raw entropy.
At the mercy of our biology, be it defecation,
or ejection of urine,
or menstrual fluids and uterine matter.
Our surroundings changing with atmospheric pressure.
The seemingly celestial and elemental measures
that impact us without provision or delivery of treasures.

Whichever scenario has the monopoly of truth,
each individual, by the close of their youth
has inevitably formed their own basis and logic
that guides their personal balancing scales.
It lays before them a series of trails
which they feel will protect them from attack, or from magic.

I construct this account to blow my own horn.
Oh, if I were able to succeed, by contortion, at that!
If it opens me up to accusation and scorn
I really don't mind, I'll chew the fat
with whomever turns up as a critic.
The racist, the antisemitic,
the fascist, the monk, the vendors of junk,

the Right-Wing, the Left, the poor and bereft,
the liar, the saint, the ugly, the quaint,
the weak and the strong and the short and the long,
the silent and loud, the meek and the proud.

CATACLYSMIC VIBRATIONS

And so, the way that I look at the world
is out of my hands.
Like all human beings, we *homo sapiens,* I have to stand
on the only two feet that I have been given.
I must observe with my only two eyes.
I must compute the landscape with my imperfect brain.
With a bent and broken weathervane.
With any assistance I am able to obtain.
Facts and opinions in an unbroken chain,
demanding that I deduce the sense
and decide what belongs on each side of the fence.

Since that morning, when I emerged from the womb,
without doubt, until I am placed in my tomb,
(that's a lie and a liberty already).
I'll be cremated - that's not a request, it's an instruction.
I have been smitten with the curse of the inquisitor.
Whether I love it, loathe it, whether I care or I don't.
Whether I want it or refuse to accept it, I won't
have any power to disown it.
It's my set-in-stone component.

Every stimulus,
visual, aural, olfactory, intellectual,
abhorrent, orgasmic, rapturous,
loving, hateful, welcome, enraging,
offensive, defensive, offended, defended,
I am unable to take it at face value.
Accept it, reject it, ignore it,
I have to pause, think, analyse and store it,
whether it pleases or disappoints.
That is the curse which determines my compass points.

CATACLYSMIC VIBRATIONS

I delve and dig to the floor of the rig.
I uncover whatever the mysteries yield,
forever, in the tri-coloured corners of the foreign field,
and the revelations of a snapping twig,
when I try to walk silently in the wood at dusk
without detection. The inhabitants hear the sounds speak,
and inquisitors lurk with the lark and the leek.

The irresistible compulsion to learn
and to seek and to soak information and skills.
An obsessional life and unstoppable urge
that can fill up the mind but can cause it to burn,
destruction, corrosion of our iron wills,
to the sound of a murmur that mimics a dirge.

The inquisitor acts as both arch enemy and loyal friend.
It is my interpretation and decisions that enact the choice.
Many years ago, from multiple teachers and sages,
I absorbed the universal wisdoms and truths, found my voice.
The fork in the road that we see at each turn, presents
two roads; less-travelled and more.
The answer is adventure, no need to keep score,
no need to think hard. No need to do more.
Let the clouds of enigma support my whole weight.
Carry my being from boredom, from blind fate,
that laser beam instinct for a blast at the unknown.

The inquisitor ate my spirit and soul,
to take ownership, conquest,
and steer me to seek and find out all secrets,
yet always aware of that prison of time and space
that will govern, and permit only that which it will.

CATACLYSMIC VIBRATIONS

That rarer road of the two offers infinite joy, when compared,
and a life filled to overflowing with dreams and with awe;
it is not to fall down as I drop to the floor.
My landing and impact are always in feathers.
Rides on the wind and the wheels of white chariots.
Thunder, wonder, the venom of the worst weathers.

Those splits in our paths, that demand that we choose,
and decide, the abundance and repetition of the obvious clues,
the orchestra will play any tunes in the world.
The baton is ours. An old tune, or the creation of a new;
I pity the fearful, and followers, and those that hide,
from a jump off the cliff and the soft feather landing below;
the quest to acquire cerebral expanse,
gluttonous feasts, parties and dance,
the creation of music, or poems, or art.
Build up a stockpile of thoughts and ideas,
find ways to share the frequencies of your heart,
threaten the safety of your complacent peers,
the inquisitor forces the brave to absorb.
To create. To express. To search. To feel.

The energy field is for all, and for real.

Ocean's End
(from 'The Ocean')

Such majesty.
That endless sea.
My mother at one with the sea and the sun.
The tears and the years, a breaking back's crack,
no turning back.

Forever with Davy Jones,
the swimmers, the drowned,
their essence invisible, all around.
Water, the element, universal, profound.

The daughter of Water.
The son of the sun.
A split of an atom by a shot from a gun.
A father's grief at the death of his son.
The unification of every soul.
Fragments coagulate, forming a whole.
The void communes as a bottomless hole.

Dreaming of flight.
Magnesium light.
A viper's bite.
The black of night.

An impossible maze.
The end of days.
Those plasma pools of imagined rules,
that we float above in schizoid schools.

CATACLYSMIC VIBRATIONS

The Fire of Aries burns my skin,
sears my being without and within,
the burns and brands attempt to win
but my gut resists with a masochist's grin.

April shine.
April wine.
April mine.
April sign.

Maternal flame.
Eternal flame.
Paternal pain.
Paternal grain.

My brittle bones are snapping
whilst the audience are clapping,
it's a spectacle of violence
and a suffering in silence,
my heart torn out and eaten
as my spine is cleaved and beaten,
the torture does not penetrate
a shield as strong as tungsten plate.
Boiling blood and melting eyes
are nothing, to my Oceansize.

Oceans of blood, of sweat and of tears
form a cushion of Air above all hopes and fears.
Aquarius screams with poison and power,
then strikes like Zeus with his thunderbolt shower.
Oceanborn child, with indigo blood,
shows wisdom and might in Isis' flood.

CATACLYSMIC VIBRATIONS

His hair is of Air.
Like Water, he sustains life everywhere,
Fire is impotent without his presence,
the inferno is tamed,
but Earth laughs at them all.
Capricorn is unashamed
to be, and know, that he will be blamed
for the limits all others must obey.
The foundations of energies that power the day.

Sailing the seven seas, the five oceans,
the one, singular, seemingly boundless ocean,
actually finite, though appearing infinite.
No Atlantic, no Pacific, Arctic, Indian, Southern,
but just one, Global, unending body of brine.
The ocean spirit of the world, under one sky.

Scorpio's sting is swift and sharp.
Libra weighs a drum and harp.
Sagittarius shoots an apple from my head.
Cancer makes certain that everyone's dead.
Leo sits patiently with Androcles,
the King of Beasts brought to his knees.

A spire, cut from Fire, marks the desire, for an empire.
The birth of the Earth, a diminuendo, the angelfire.
Seven chakras align through a spinal cord,
A Kundalini serpent guards a priceless hoard,
Water and Air cast a spell forged from light.
The Pylons of Set hold the secrets of night.

Taurus charges with marauding pace.
Virgo smiles with unrivalled grace.
Pisces swims in Oceanic glory.
Gemini tells both sides of the story.

**(For Mum, Patricia Anne Watkins, Fire of Aries.
10 April 1945 - 20 June 2019)**

Albatross

You are my Ancient Mariner,
world-weary, long-suffering,
painfully alone in the midst of a sea of people.

Your own world contains so many heavy weights.
They stay invisible, often, until you tell me.
Intuition was never my strongest suit.

And when you do tell me about them,
it can sometimes be
from a place of vulnerability,
but when it's not,
there is a cornered leopard before me.

Yes, I know it's all my fault.
When you make me aware of it,
and when you don't,
either way I am often already aware.

The questions, the seeds,
of the imminent development
of black thunderclouds overhead,
begin to open out
in uncontrollable and searing tones.

Do I try to listen, peacefully?
Do I walk away, and away, and away,
as far as I can in a single day?
Do I hide in the broom cupboard,

even though we don't have one?
Do I bounce the blame
off the impervious wall,
as if it were a rubber ball,
at the exasperation of your inner child?

Bearing pain that builds and builds
like Christ's on the cross,
I know what I am;
your albatross.

Now, I sit in the car,
in an arbitrarily selected thinking place,
a parking space,
scribbling, on a scrappy pad,
my inadequate declaration of apology,
hoping it can be accepted and not excepted,
hoping it is met with kindness
instead of its deserved cold rejection,
because this mess is self-inflicted.

Are my body and form expanding,
or is it just the time advancing,
that make me grow heavier?
I'm concentrating when I should be patient and calm.

Patient, and calm,
to free my guilt and sorrow
from watering the roots of this exile,
to find the most appropriate language
to convey my sincerest humility.
But the void will not raise its barrier,
so I remain in my freezing tomb.

I clutch at temporary forgiveness today,
knowing that I am growing
forever heavier,
hour by hour, day by day,
around your sweet neck,
toward the moment when you can take no more,
and have to release me.
You'll let me go
and I'll drop, without hope, stranded,
to the floor.

A Game of Chess

I

The alchemists' dream to turn Lead into Gold
was never that clever, if truth be told.
You'd soon hum a tune by your mountain of yellow,
saying "now there's no Lead!"
you'd be a sad fellow.
An inversion as simple as Yang into Yin,
or through your front door
when without walks within.

(nods to Edgar Allan Poe)

II

A Raven, a door
to the lovely Lenore,
brushing her hair
with catatonic stare.

An Owl with a trowel
and a looseness of bowel,
leaves a guanic trail,
like the slime of a snail,
or the conflicts of phlegm
of an 'Us' or a 'Them'.

CATACLYSMIC VIBRATIONS

What's the form of the norm?
To disguise or surprise?
Neither, or both?
Gluttony or Lust?
Joy or disgust?

Or to wake up at dawn,
in the moist early morn,
with a raging of horn?

III

I have a pain.
Inside my brain.
It's a chilblain.
There's heavy rain.
Can't complain.
Is it a bird?
Is it a plane?
A lion's mane?
A wanky stain?
A wagon train?

That heavy rain, is it D_2O?
Deuterium, to confuse them all.
Is there acid in it, Yes or No?
Alkaline liquid down the wall.
Litmus tests on a country lane.
Full of scavenging rats and a rolling ball.
Raindrops race down a windowpane.
Torrents deluge one and all.
Sun-ray's rainbow can't contain

This blitz within its modest squall.
Its laser burn, its arched domain.

IV

It's the Twelfth Night of Christmas,
and Malvolio has missed us.
The most tempestuous aerial
bombardment and burial,
premature but perfect.
The Lisbon and the Maastricht.

A European Edgar,
an Edward, an Elgar,
a William, a Shaker,
a mover, a maker.

An unbearable lightness,
a blackness, a whiteness,
a darkness, a lightness.

Three witches curse the Crown.
A dynasty cut cruelly down
and castles crumble to the ground.

Toby Belches yellow bile,
it burns the chequered parlour tile.

Face aglow with puce and scarlet,
lecherous drools at the harlot.
Her name is Charlotte.

Our Juliet and our Romeo
as close as Love and Death can go,
poor Romeo, poor Juliet,
the classic, tragic epithet.

Chess is, of course,
a war metaphor.
Strategic, tactical,
the ultimate score,
horrific to be forced
to concede a draw.
A stalemate,
a log jam,
and glue on the floor.

V

This chess game has a twisted curse;
it couldn't be worse.
Black goes first.

Why the Scarlet Unicorn?
A watching pawn.
Watching porn.

He has a seat on the board.
Peaceful, but bored.
A piece on the board.

What's the name of that concubine?
It's Columbine.
I like her shine.

CATACLYSMIC VIBRATIONS

I'm sure I see a daisy chain.
It looks like Spain.
In the rain.

It falls mainly on the plain.
A charmed refrain.
To entertain.

The Bishop wears a mitre hat.
A metric mat.
Under that.

The Knight's tale tells
of magic spells.
Chiming bells.

Rook moves straight, or up and down,
a ferocious frown
takes you down.

There is no doubt about who's King,
meandering
with a ball of string.

For a second, he's about to sing,
the weirdest thing,
a singing King.

The Queen has majesty and grace.
A smiling face.
Knows her place.

A Jubilee to end them all.
Take down the wall.
Change it all.

**"Money can't buy happiness" they say.
But you can. If you give it away.**

BBC (Britain and BrylCreem)

The power, the glory,
the front-page story,
a splintered furore of scattering shards;
stammering, stuttering,
choking and spluttering,
scooting and scuttling for inches and yards.

In bundling; in trundling;
the banners, the bunting,
the hounding and hunting will open the gates.

Inside is a spectre,
an orb and a sceptre,
a crown with its lustre and clusters of crates.

The map of the route
to a tree and a root
has been charred and compressed,
impaled and impressed,
produced and provided pastiche and applause,
but harpies a-screeching, ramming and reaching,
will lay down and raise the effect from the cause.

Cantankerous cunts,
resplendent but runts;
circumstance and pomp,
hypocritical hearts.

CATACLYSMIC VIBRATIONS

Undies undone;
spider's web underspun;
the spear and the gun,
desperation departs.

Armageddon arrives.
Urticaria hives
in the houses of war,
of mushroom and spore,
beneath and behind,
unravel, unwind,
the bastards browbeaten like never before.

Is this revolution?
Is this the DeWitts?
Is this the Bastille?
The castles in flames?
The fall of the empire?
The fire of the flags?
The removal of leaders?
The erasing of names?

Don't get so excited.
It's England. It's eggs.
It's stiff upper lips.
It's dribbles and dregs.
Breakfast and bacon,
toasties and tea;
football and farting;
"you looking at me?"

National Health Service?
Pay for your stuff!

America decided
enough was enough.
Everyone's buying,
everything's for sale,
raffle your child and
The Holy F...... Grail.

Blighty and Boris.
Thatcher and Blair.
Britain and bulldogs,
Corgis and crap.
Cricket and Royals,
croquet and grass;
your TV Licence?
Right up your arse.

Hateful. Spiteful.
Racist police.
Keeping in line,
not keeping the peace.
"Do as I told you,
stand over there,
don't eyeball me, son.
Sit in that chair."

"Toby, naughty,
have you been bad?
Do you want a coffee?
I'll just call your Dad.
Anything in your pockets?
A quarter of hash?
Let's just share a spliff,
go home with your stash."

CATACLYSMIC VIBRATIONS

The BBC News,
black girls and suits;
scripted to perfection,
slick 'autocutes'.
Let's talk to our expert
in Foreign Affairs;
a BBC Oxbridge
who's Brylcreemed his hairs.

Gareth knows rugby,
brought up in Wales,
check out his accent,
he's from Ebbw Vale.
He knows how the scrum works;
"over to yous!"
Pub laddie banter
on BBC News.

You know you can trust them,
"go get your jab!"
It's all in the science.
Made in a lab.
Don't read the small print,
they did all the trials;
we're the BBC!
Sofas and smiles.

This man's a doctor.
Look at his graph!
A brainy boffin.
Knows what's in your barf.

He'll explain all the details
(or that's how it looks),
you can tell from his voice that he's read all the books.

The experts all work for the BBC too
(the ones that are usually on BBC2)
editor of this, correspondent for there,
men that wear suits and have Brylcreemed their hair.

The beautiful Beeb that you've watched all your life.
Part of the furniture. Safe as your wife.
The word 'propaganda' is carefully used,
for countries we already know are Bad Nows.
You won't ever hear it describing our friends,
as that wouldn't fit with the means or the ends.

Do I sound like a cynic?
A bearer of lies?
Distrustful unjustly?
Jaded? Unwise?
Perhaps I should learn to embrace compromise.
But if I did that, where's the chance of surprise?

Do you switch on the telly by pressing the '1'?
Is that just the thing that you've generally done?
Habits are formed in just twenty-one days.
You'll have them for ever. You'll live in the maze.
Habits are broken in just three weeks too.
I am living proof that it's easy to do.
Breaking the chains of a routine so numb
is as simple as learning to (not) suck your thumb.

CATACLYSMIC VIBRATIONS

What would you do if you suddenly had time?
Would you indulge in political rhyme?
Perhaps not. But you would have things you would do.
How many kids do you have? One or two?

Do you know who is in charge of your life?
Who makes the rules? The trouble, the strife.
You can decide what you do, what you see;
or delegate that to the ol' BBC.

If you did the 'three weeks' I will promise you this.
You would not return to the televised bliss.
You'd find magic moments in every day.
You'd choose when to work, when to rest, when to play.

And if you mistakenly watch the TV,
you'll laugh to yourself as you notice you're free.
The sight of the news will deliver a shock,

as you see right through time

with a different clock.

The Wrath of Mars
(The X Mantra. 6 x 6)

The Bringer of Harm.
The Bringer of Woe.
The Bringer of Calamity.
The Bringer of Destruction.
The Bringer of Death.
The Bringer of Annihilation.

The Spirit of Darkness.
The Spirit of Elimination.
The Spirit of Chaos.
The Spirit of Vacuum.
The Spirit of Void.
The Spirit of Antimatter.

The Essence of Nothingness.
The Essence of Evil.
The Essence of Hatred.
The Essence of Spite.
The Essence of Dread.
The Essence of Horror.

The Intention to Terrify.
The Intention to Mortify.
The Intention to Purify.
The Intention to Chastify.
The Intention to Fibrofy.
The Intention to Dystrophy.

The Will to Waste.
The Will to Kill.
The Will to Burn.
The Will to Fry.
The Will to Sear.
The Will to Boil.

The Wrath of Flesh.
The Wrath of Flame.
The Wrath of Heat.
The Wrath of Hate.
The Wrath of Man.
The Wrath of Mars.

Sapio-Crush
(dedicated to Elon Musk)

To call someone a genius, most of the time,
is to speak of a trajectory in a linear line.
On an Einsteinian plane, or in Nietzsche's brain,
or an LSD trip in McKenna's domain,
or Mozart, even when going insane.

They dig the one hole, but they dig it so deep,
while the rest of humanity wanders like sheep,
or flirts with commitment in an unconscious sleep.

I'm a sapiophile, which I'm proud to announce,
so I'm tough to impress, by the pound or the ounce.

There's a man in our midst that is light years ahead,
this awe in my verse almost quivers with dread,
at the scope of the hope of the future to come,
like the sheer other-worldliness of Gartzka's drum.
PayPal was the catalyst, Stepping Stone One.

Musk is the name, I say it like Bond,
like a legendary figure from a Grecian pond.
A focused laser, an unstoppable force,
thinks in ten dimensions at the pace of a horse,
as if every second of life must be sapped,
every priceless moment, captured and trapped.

His only restraint, the finiteness of time,
ironically an abstract paradigm.

CATACLYSMIC VIBRATIONS

Pioneering spirit of its truest kind,
had seemed to be lost in the modern mind,
then suddenly and gradually at the same time,
a man found ways to invert said paradigm.

Instead of answering just one question,
he batters everything into submission.
One, to the next, to the next, to the next,
as if burn-out's the challenge, the prescribed pretext.

A Sahara of panels to power all Earth,
already, in his wake, true electric car birth.
Dragon after dragon, slain by pure drive,
is there any adversary that's worthy, alive?

Never in history such an animal seen,
creating and storming the gates of the spleen.
Tunnels of freeways, under the ground,
billions in the bank don't slow the pace down.
If anything, this accelerates the speed
of this one-in-a-zillion carnivore's feed.

Tesla was clever, but Musk is the man,
the improviser of a masterful plan.
Elon's the enigma at the top of the tree,
landing a rocket on a mat in the sea,
but he never says "I", he always says "we"

The moral of the story, there isn't one.
Just pointing out something under the sun.
Fusion of technical and human goals
are as rare as a diamond, and as hot as its coals.

There's somebody trying, and managing to,
a new Robin Hood, and his aim is true.
A man to whom cash is just a means to an end,
an end that might see off the greed and transcend.

The Philosopher

There was rumoured to be a man
that had lived for more than three hundred years.

It was said he lived near the summit of a mountain, in a cave.

Nobody knew how long he had been there,
or where he came from.

He had blankets for warmth,
and a cup to catch rainwater.

The birds would fly up, up and up,
and stay with him, to talk of life, of dreams, of light and of truth.

The birds would bring him food, though often they would bring
too much, and he would feed them
back with what was left over.

Legend tells of his wisdom and of his eight 'eyes':
insight, intellect, instinct, intuition,
intelligence, imagination, inspiration, and integrity.

"Everything that is and that is not can be seen with those",
he would say.

It was felt that everyone should try and spend some time in his
company at least once in their life.

In fact, it was said that he was happy to speak with

anyone that wished to speak with him.
As long as they were happy to climb the mountain.

It seemed worthwhile to me, to climb the mountain
and meet this man at the very top of the world.

It is wonderful discovering how easy it can be
to climb a high mountain,
when the anticipation and the aim are so equally lofty.

Along my journey towards the mountain I met many people.

I would ask each traveller whether they had spoken
with the old man.

"Yes, of course" they would always answer.

I would then ask, "how many times have you been to see him?"

"Once! For two reasons; one, it is such a difficult climb
that the thought of going up twice is highly unattractive,
and two, you stay with him
until you have exhausted all your questions,
so once is enough.

I took the trip to the cave.
As I entered, he looked at me and smiled
as if we had known each other all my life.

I was soon to find out that we had,
though not in any human way.

He asked me to sit with him, on the floor, facing him.

I felt an urge to swear,
as if he were a school friend that wouldn't care.

"This place is so fucking high up! More than I expected."

"It is never necessary to use a swear word",
he said with quiet gravity.
"It is an indicator of weakness, disrespect and low character".

I could tell he felt no offence,
and did not want or expect me to apologise.

It felt calm and reassuring that I was about to learn from him.

"What is the meaning of life?" I asked,
thinking I had may as well
start with the big one. "Is there one?"

The chuckle he let free was that of a man
who had fully expected
that to be my first question –
like it was everybody's first question.
Yet he was politely amused rather than bored by it.

He had also not shown disapproval at my rudeness,
in asking a second question before
allowing him to answer the first.
A lot of people ask two questions at once.
"Not just one, no" he replied, knowingly.
Immediately, certainly, having been asked
tens of thousands of times.
"It has more than ten thousand meanings.
Each woman or man lives by,

and follows the path of,
different combinations of them."

"We strive for happiness, some more than others.
We strive for a sense of purpose,
a sense of success.
A sense of worth, in human terms.
The joy of giving to others,
and feeling the warmth of receiving
the love and appreciation of those others.

The Japanese call it **Ikigai**."

Ikigai is the concept of living a life of purpose, happiness, service and worth.

He looked through me, as if to touch my soul.

"Release is the gateway to peace".

"Possession is the gateway to obsession".

I understood, as I physically absorbed
the energy he was sharing with me

"Tell me of Woman"
were the next words that uttered themselves.

His gaze, which was already serene and calm,
softened still further.
His voice became a murmur and a whisper.
"Woman is a much higher being than Man.
She grasps the layered energies of the world

from a deeper, yet more elevated, perspective.

Woman is engaged with Spirit more naturally than Man.
Her chemicals, her hormones, give rise to
inclusive rather than exclusive emotions.

Woman does not drop and default to aggression
in the ways that Man does.

Man's violent thoughts are meant for protective purposes,
but he often misunderstands his own mind, and so
misuses and abuses his powers and gifts.

He gets lost.
Woman is the guardian of the emotional map."

(To be continued… perhaps)

Assertion of Self

The hustle and bustle of the planet was silenced,
a momentous move, by a little bitty microbe.
Its invisible, immeasurable, immense impact
as it jumped over our vulnerable lives
like a portentous grasshopper,
almost without sound save the giveaway,
unmistakable rasp of the scraping of wing on leg.

It can be difficult for an untrained ear to differentiate
between the grasshopper and the cricket.
But, whichever it is that's within earshot,
one is reminded of the humid warmth
of the British summer and a fragrant thicket,
pacing down a Yorkshire snicket,
inhaling deeply to ingest aromas of wildflowers.

Do we now view our lives
through the old prism or the new,
or an alloy of the two?
Perhaps the picture will reveal itself as time plods on.

Where does one look in order to see accuracy of image?
Purity rather than preparation.
Where does one read an unadulterated word?
Where is the truth to be witnessed or heard?

That walk in the woods is a sanctified space,
beyond the reach of devious spin,

beyond the doctors of content
and bastardised, weaponised alteration.

A pillow of blissful imagination
where the senses can lie,
so far from gogglebox and potter's wheel,
so far from stainless knives of Sheffield steel,
slicing and dicing our processed meal.

It was many years hence
that the foul taste of bitter pills
drove the pure of heart to disengage;
every word a lie,
or a frame of careful construction,
or a Weapon of Mass Destruction,
thank you, sirs, and madams,
at the British Broadcasting Corporation.

We walked and turned away, to a cleaner day,
where the clearer way is in view.
We can see straight through.
No muck on the panes,
no fog in the brains,
you can see, and breathe, and weave.

In a meadow,
carpeted in buttercup and dandelion yellow,
daisy white. I need peace. I need light.
I'm falling through an intrunsicated crack
in the parquet floor,
where I can see the intellectual fire
of raw wisdom, surrounded
by what appears to be a pneumatic tyre.

CATACLYSMIC VIBRATIONS

Let me return to that twilight,
get in the zone, let me be alone.
Please.
Release me from the bond.
I'm afraid of all this, I don't know
what my thoughts are telling me to do.
The messages are all in code,
confusing, broken, like mash-up music.

Let me understand.
I'm dreaming of a distant land,
one where I fly, high, merged with sky.
My body undefined, unrefined, undermined
by swooping swallows diving upon me.

Let me see, let me know, let me show you my fear,
let me let you see every last tear
that falls from my stinging eyes.
Let me rise,
let my imagination run
in the direction of the sun.
Let me be one.
Set me free, to just be. Yes, let me be.

Where is the focus? The frame?
The clarity? The charity?
Is it possible to feel the form
of the re-ordering of the mess,
the chaos, the stress.

Where's the show? Can I go? Do you even know?
I've got my subconscious babblings in tow….
they go where they go.

CATACLYSMIC VIBRATIONS

It's as simple as that,
you don't get to dissect me
and distil my stern mystery
into its components,
for your amusement, or for anyone's.

Morphing, drifting and flying on a magic carpet
I am returned to the humidity of the moorland,
and falling ever so slowly and gently
onto a mattress of marshmallow
and into a lucid waking dreamscape.

I am finding me, where I have always been
and reclaiming my awareness of my
true, settled self from the nomadic self
that was at the rudder of my
edgy discomfort and psychedelic travels,
at the nadir of the fear of system control
and injections of experimental concoctions.
I disown that invasion and intervention
into my sacred space.
Into me.

Dropping, falling, plummeting down into me.
I recognise the safety and protection that encases me,
in this ball of fire at my spiritual core,
where there are no tangible, intangible or existential threats,
as if I'm a turtle, tortoise, or coiled armadillo
with an impenetrable shell.

It looks like this, this bliss, this universal kiss
of armoured intimacy and ultimacy.

CATACLYSMIC VIBRATIONS

My being is an indestructible rock
of untouchable diamond
and cataclysmic heat,
to incinerate any invader,
I have all-consuming protection and security.

At last I can bathe in the multiversal energies,
empty my mind of reality,
and disintegrate to become the oneness.

Is there anything more to know?
I don't know.
Let me go.

I Determine

Every second is new.
A choice.
A decision.
A determination.
A moment of fresh, free, will.

A minute, an hour,
a succession of carriages
of a time-train,
each lived, experienced
and immediately destroyed,
never to return, repeat,
reappear, re-exist.

The train stops, starts and travels where I choose.
The direction; the velocity and the acceleration,
I determine everything.

Half of the scientists, and
half of the philosophers, and
half of the pragmatists, and
half of the dreamers,
half of the artists, and
half of the poets, and
half of the planners, and
half of the thinkers,
say there are no choices,

or decisions
or freedoms
or controls,
just predetermined fate.

We are merely passengers on the train of time
if you ask that half of humanity.

I determine,
argue and assert, that
I am driving my train.
I have the other half of humanity
accompanying me,
on my magical
journey of discovery,
we determine where we go, and when,
with our hands on our steering wheels,
our feet on the throttles and brakes,
and the wind of our thoughts at our backs.
No-one is really aware which assessment
of this life of ours owns the facts.

Does it matter?

To me, yes it does,
whether I run the show,
whether it's possible to know,
I stop, and I go,
I believe, and so,
I am empowered by my illusion.

Anxiety and Depression
(High Density ADHD)

Anxiety and Depression.
Do they belong together or not
in the mental health melting pot, with
Insanity, Obsession & Sobriety?
Adios….

A lachrymal flood cascading,
crimson blood flowing,
like semen, coming before it is going.

I'm strong, but that's wrong.
I'm shy, but that's a lie.
I'm smart, in my heart.
I'm thick, in my dick.
I try not to die, but that's tough when it's rough.
Hear me when I shout!
I have things to let out,
the nectar she produces,
such sweet, fragrant juices.

It's all such a muddle,
I just want a cuddle,
to feel safe, or feel well,
or both, I can't tell.
Life is a garden, my thoughts are the seeds.
I choose what I plant there, flowers or weeds.
What we plant is what grows.
We reaps what we sows.

CATACLYSMIC VIBRATIONS

I need a bright flare.
Not this black nightmare.
It's too frightening.
Send me lightning.
Burn out my eyes, burn out my heart,
burn out the end, burn out the start,
burn me alive, burn my dead corpse,
burn up my spirit, while my soul warps.

My in-tray is full of horseshit and bull.
I can't fail to see they're all lying to me.
Be it ITV or the BBC.
That look in their eyes, of transparent lies.
Wherever I turn there's deceit in the churn.
It's easy to tell from the godawful smell.
Do I hide, inside, my cave?
Or scream, be bold, be brave?

Shall I open a vein?
Bleed out in the rain?
Has enough been done?
Will I roast in the sun?

A cocktail of drugs?
A noose on a tree?
Does it honestly matter
what happens to me?
A drop in the ocean.
Perpetual motion.
A piss in the sea.
A shit in the earth.
There's no calibration of anyone's worth.

Affection, love,
an olive, a dove,
below, above.
I need to feed my greed
with cash or dope or speed.

The lights are fading,
all brightness is shading,
my rainbow has gone
from where the sun shone.

The only colour I see
is the blackening of me.
I just need a spark,
I'm scared of the dark,
I drown in this fear,
I don't want to be here,

I want to be there, on the greener grass,
where the Billy Goats' Gruff are free to pass.

The Weirdness of it

Life.

It's just a thing,
a thing we all do,
a thing we all are.
We do the same things, on occasion,
but in different ways,
and we do, on other occasions, different things.

Would you like to read of my little life?

If not, you'll need to avert your gaze
and your concentration,
because my story follows, at this location.

I did the same thing as you, mostly, initially.
I popped out of a belly.
No Julius Caesar involved, in my case,
nor any other emperor, or other place.
Crawled around, pulled myself up
on pieces of furniture, learned to stand,
gaining courage to walk without a hand
on the walls, or the chairs, flying solo.

Realised along the way that all the noises
and mumbles I heard, were language.
Communication. The power of it!
Instinct only, at the time,
no idea of the weight of it,

the weaponry of it,
or what occult laws were held within it.

Mastering the abilities of the limbs.
Mastering the abilities of the fingers.
Throwing things, thumping things,
thinking things, and through the thoughts,
finding out the rules of the big game.
There are these 'senses', I found,
seeing Sight, detecting Smell, tasting Taste, feeling Touch,
Hearing sound;
trust those weird-shaped ears to need a second syllable.

The tricks would all uncover themselves
slowly, but ever so surely,
how and when to use them all,
and what could be achieved
if each were used at the right times
and in the right proportions.
Or the left.

Understanding the brains, and the brawn,
and, of course, the wisdom to know the difference.
Then the dominance, either by brawn or by brain,
or with the dexterity of mind and hand
working in tandem.
Picking fights.
Winning fights.
Losing fights.
Learning that every outcome contained a lesson.

Learning the lessons.
Loving the lessons.

Acting on the learning.
Observing.
Calculating.
Computing.
Strategy.
Tactics.

The right friends, the wrong friends,
oftentimes those that were both.
Teachers and teachings of life,
teachers and teachings at school.
Being good at football, scoring goals,
brought kudos and celebrity
within that one colossal cosmos, in a single building.
Respect from boys,
kisses from girls.
Being clever, but careful to
exercise discretion with the intellect.
To use or not to use.
Hands up; hands down.

Nobody likes a swot;
especially if it's all you've got;
but the brain does a lot more
than sums, and skills in writing,
when the prizes are so inviting.

The Triangle, the Triquetra, the Pyramid,
clear sight of the summit,
method and manner of climbing,
manipulation, Machiavelli and magnetism,
mastery, mischief and misbehaviour.

CATACLYSMIC VIBRATIONS

Selfishness, naturally, but also teamwork;
leadership, obviously, but with allegiances and loyalty.
Friendship creates and assists that royalty.
One battles and bumbles through.

As children and adolescents
we are all but immortal beings,
no grip on or concept of time,
no technical reason or rhyme
or the rational bells they can chime.
Perpetually riding sublime
on waves and tides, with selected partners in crime.
The rites of passage.
The smashing of windows,
the doorstep thefts of milk,
shouting and squealing in classrooms to see
if Sir could spin around fast enough
to catch me, or maybe, thee.
But they were never that quick,
and it made them fucking sick.
Sir, you can suck my dick.

Shoplifting sweets in Woolworths, after school,
worth their weight in plutonium,
not that we had a clue what that was,
or how many people you can kill with it.
7" vinyl records, they cost nearly a pound,
so, for those, the criminal skills had to be sound.

Adulation from the cronies
felt like adulthood.
Such insignificant triumphs,

but they felt like Olympic gold,
which we'd have naively sold.
When you're in such a tiny pond
being a big fish is a big deal.
Looking back now, everything's a blur,
years seem like flashes of lightning,
nothing sustains as frightening,
we were invincible, indestructible warriors.
We were going to live forever and be kings.
Kings of the world, of time, of space,
everything a competition, a race.

Mortality though, is a creeping enemy,
as inevitable as time itself, if time is real,
fears and realities that one cannot steal,
they're not sweets, nor are they even sweet.
Whether we are the greatest, or least,
it follows, and it gains,
it seems slow - but no - it is relentless, it burns,
and it never turns.
And so, we don't need to turn, and check.
It's felt, every instant, by those hairs on the neck.

My first true encounter with the march of fate
came as fast as an angry bull from a gate;
at 29 years old, at the top of the world,
came the fall to the depths of the dimensional bowels.
They used to call us mad.
They didn't understand it,
they didn't understand me when it came my way,
and they still have no idea today.

CATACLYSMIC VIBRATIONS

It scares them all, as it damned well should,
for it wears anonymity under a pitch-black hood.
It decided, with what seemed random, vicious spite,
to land on my psyche like a spirit of night.
The Hammer of Thor,
to obliterate my narcissistic spirit from sight.
My schizophrenia had dropped by,
to say a cheeky, naughty "hi".
They called it, the first time around,
as if to goad my arrogant inner scamp,
a psychotic episode, a visiting clown,
as in "you'll be right as rain, champ".
The medication changes once in a while.
The relapses descend and strike once in a while.
A stay in a psychiatric ward is a great leveller,
like molasses poured over a turbo-propeller.
The bloated salary doomed to the past.
A crow's nest empty atop a broken mast.

A few years later in 2009,
bolt from the blue, number two.
My mind began to whirl - a vertigo swirl.
Unable to walk. My legs just went, gave way.
Having to crawl to the toilet.
Confusion is not the word, it was terror.
And bafflement, no balance. How? What?
Out of nowhere.
It felt worse than the psycho-attack, it was physical.
My face was numb, on one side.
What is happening? Is this me in a wheelchair? Or The End?
After days, of delays, of misdiagnosis,

as I'd become ill on the eve of a Bank Holiday weekend.
Is this the stars, or a god, inflicting punishment,
for all that testosterone in my youth?
Someone tell me the fucking truth…………..
It's definitely not a stroke,
said four junior doctors, each with their certainty.
On the Tuesday morning,
the stroke specialist picked up a steel stapler
and touched me all over with it,
hot or cold?
hot or cold?
hot or cold?
"You've had a stroke.
Cerebellum, left stem."
The falseness of those mirages, illusions of eternal life
had again been perfectly demonstrated.

The weirdness, shocks, and surprises of the unfolding of life
are shadows that are always at my side, like an unloved wife.
Inescapable, haunting my shoulder,
like a ghost, an angel, a devil, as I try to grow older.
As we all advance in years,
through the laughter, the tears,
our understanding grows with us,
we look back, beyond clouds and fog.
We might live with a cat, or a dog,
a budgerigar, a hamster, even a TV,
me, I still have loved ones with me.
And I have loved ones that have gone.
A scarred heart from its breakages,
blessings to count, in an amount
I have scarcely deserved.

CATACLYSMIC VIBRATIONS

I have no illusions any more,
not even of celestial gates,
or a supernatural door.
I do not look forward with any dread
at that beckoning day of the dead.

You would think that if there were a god
he'd have had his fun with me by now!
Did I screw up so badly, at this life thing?
Deserving the misfortunes?
Well, either way, there's more.
Something I had never heard of before.
Perhaps not as worthy of fear
as the previous afflictions catalogued here.
I began losing weight, and muscle mass,
and this one has an official name too,
but for a schizophrenic,
it's thankfully a cinch to remember,
they call it sarcopenia,
from the Greek words for 'flesh', and 'poverty'.
I mean, how cute is that?
'Muscle atrophy',
is another term for that.
At least I'm not going to get fat,
no matter how much crap I shovel down.

In all the excitement along the way,
perhaps to prevent me from writing all day,
I forgot to explain the diabetes, type 2.
It's just more tablets, I take so many,
at least I get help that saves me a penny.

CATACLYSMIC VIBRATIONS

A gastric issue, to mention in passing,
side effects of drugs that are rather embarrassing,
I rattle away like a diamondback,
to send warnings ahead as I trudge down the track.
I think you'll agree that my story's unique.
But so is yours, and so is everybody's.
Plans. Luck. Actions whose consequences are not visible.
Like I said at the start,
for some, it's their heart,
a crash of a car,
too long in a bar,
a rare new disease,
mixed in with sleazo.
A tumour. A stroke.
A decision to smoke. And never bothering to stop.
Nobody's afraid of me now
any more than when I would
deceive myself that they were.

It's the weirdness of it all
that makes the unpredictable voyage
just so exhilarating,
and so overwhelmingly, spectacularly beautiful.

If only we could take another turn
on the merry-go-round, with fairground sounds
that some all-powerful, curious boy
could wind up, as his clockwork toy.

CATACLYSMIC VIBRATIONS

The Black Death?

Darkness approaches
swarms of cockroaches
nibbling at my heart
it's a masterpiece of art
an avalanche of memories
flash flood of my contemporaries
singing cherubim and crows
the fearshadow grows
dark matter absorbs
in a shower of orbs
light fights with the dark
bloodscent to a shark
my essence in fade
the towering shade
my energy failing
the schooner is sailing
my dwindling detection
of mad insurrection
advancing upon
all the sunrays that shone
before the lifeforce had gone
I'm weakened and faint
no sinner, no saint
no choir with a blessing
my spirit transgressing
my soul transcends
but I can't make amends
like the fall of Macbeth
on a cyclone of death

CATACLYSMIC VIBRATIONS

I can feel it enclosing
all senses composing
a symphonic screamer
to deafen this dreamer
what remains of myself
are the chains of my self
that I'm trying to feel
although none of it's real
or sublime or surreal
I dissolve in a mist
of a clenched, desperate fist
can I access my will
am I cognisant still
am I ether alone
no skin and no bone
not liquid nor gas
disembodied mass
awareness evaporating
departure extrapolating
destiny in control
not a part, not a whole
I asked all my days
what lies past this haze
any hint of a gaze
from a being, a force
a goddess, some remorse
humility, let go
of that shallow ego
so fragile and weak
I'm unable to speak
I am thought, I am air
I am everywhere

CATACLYSMIC VIBRATIONS

I'm nowhere, I'm gone
yet still I move on
the power explodes
in esoteric nodes
that soulless conundrum
the mystical fulcrum
protruding through time
through reason, through rhyme
through pattern, through line
through veins that entwine
up a galactic spine
via engines that whine
I spread far and wide
inside the outside
there's feeling, there's not
like a heroin shot
or a mushroom trip
or a shamanic flip
to an Ayahuasca wave
am I damned or saved
or in a limbo or dream
in a psilocybin stream
is this a consciousness peak
a continuous streak
does it end, does it stop
does it rise, does it drop
will I understand or just fly
is there earth, is there sky
is there anything to grasp
is it going to pass
does oblivion come
does it rattle or hum

CATACLYSMIC VIBRATIONS

will I reincarnate
in a whirlpool of fate
ascension, reverse
a diabolical curse
have I any control
am I in a black hole
is this how they work
is the cosmos berserk
is it order or chaos
will our history betray us
punished by karma
for all of our drama
no way to escape
every mistake, every scrape
let me out of this ride
show me the 'other side'
that we hear of in songs
of rights and of wrongs
I want answers now
the why and the how
the evidence, the proof
the lies and the truth
the mystery explained
the philosophy framed
revelations revealed
constants congealed
eyes opened wide
treasures inside
the chambers' doors
the pregnant pause
all wisdom and folly
the ivy, the holly

the confusion and the clarity
the crimes and the charity
the faith and the hope
the breadth and the scope
put me out of my doubt
must I panic and shout
we assume when we die
that the secrets float by
or the void eats our being
at the end of our seeing
a climax and more
behind the last door

Trickle

When you kissed him, you didn't realise I saw.
You kissed him like you hadn't kissed me before.
A cut appeared, spontaneously,
at the tip of my thumb.
My lifeblood, my ichor, dripping
with but a minimum of momentum.

But as the crocodile would gain on Smee,
the grimmest of reapers was following me.
Essence disappearing down a drain,
gone forever, so purposefully,
like the sea absorbing the invisible rain.

Ever so slowly and yet surely,
the drops and trickles undo me.
Your catalyst of a kiss destroys me.
Malevolently, malignantly.

As I grow weaker, and weaker,
as eyesight blurs, and fades away,
my thumb still open, and now pouring,
no longer a small, steady drip,
but flowing and growing.

I now know how a plant or flower dries and dies
without water or air,
I know how it feels
when the glow of happiness becomes raw despair.

That kiss, unimportant to you,
withering my being, just from my seeing,
smashing the understanding of what is true
and the foundations of my vision of you.

I'll die by instalments, no will to survive,
no way to return, regroup, be alive.
My body is bloodless. One cut was enough.
Sufficient to end me; time does its stuff.

A COVID Ode

I'm off to Newcastle, to purchase some coal,
I'm digging my garden, to make a deep, dark hole.
I'm scared of that Omicron on the BBC,
and the Alpha and the Delta on the ITV.

'Government briefings' of relentless hype.
Tabloid announcements in front page type.
Quaxxine commercials like laser beams.
YouTube deletions by the 'Fact Check' teams.

COVID mutates every time we blink,
and it needs much more than the kitchen sink,
we must have a jab every time that we're told,
as it seems so much worse than a Common Cold
or a bout of Flu, a splutter or sneeze,
it's the Big Pandemic, a deadly disease.

If I don't act fast and ask, "how high?"
when ordered to jump, I'm going to die.
My natural immunity won't be enough.
Even if my constitution is tough.

I need more jabs! So does my child!
This terrible virus is scampering wild!

Do not listen to those that do not believe!
It's not an opinion like Remain versus Leave!
The media gave us our Brexit wet dream!
Pharmaceutical shares are the Fat Cats' cream.

CATACLYSMIC VIBRATIONS

They kept it 'schtum', the 'emergency use',
or the vaccine drive might have looked like abuse.
But it's 'The Science', therefore it cannot be wrong,
"I did my research" so my knowledge is strong;
a 'Conspiracy Theorist' if I disagree,
(a term invented to discredit me).

Where's that Professor's lecture I share
on my Facebook page? It now isn't there.
It's disappeared, I can't post for a week,
I inherit the Earth, but am unable to speak,
on social media I'm rendered the meek,
insignificant, cancelled, fragile and weak.

It's a Propaganda War, let's make no mistake,
but see the Ivory Towers start to crumble and quake.

The secrets are out. The lies are exposed.
The BBC suits, all calm and composed,
that tell us the truth (but only a portion)
to try and pretend that there's no dark distortion.

Nothing hidden. Nothing withheld.
Transparent. The Truth. Trustworthy.

SELLED.

(......."Sold" doesn't rhyme. Dammit.)

Dust and Ashes

On some days, I sense that I am
swimming in salamander soup.
Salamander, rhubarb and egg.
The laughing sleep, and crying pain,
the projections on the wall,
imagery and recognisable horror,
escape behind a hexagonal mirror
and the teardrops of time.

Released, untethered, as if to undo
a Gordian Knot of tangled memory;
or Pythagoras, dreaming in
the central chamber of trapped souls,
calculating wisdom, balance,
and deceitful but enlightened awe.

A flying aspidistra, in a greenhouse, full of gases
and the creeping goo of molasses,
of treacle, of magnetic attraction,
of quantifiable, quantum mechanical machines.
A decree from the immaturity of
narcissistic deities, conceited, hidden.

Scrambled for disguise,
eyes, fixed forward in an iron gaze;
a coal mine canary, lost in a tree-maze,
imagined and vague
or a crumb of worthless absolution?

CATACLYSMIC VIBRATIONS

Prayer, and pride, devouring inside,
malignant in management
of the Statue of Justice,
with its blindness or vision of eternity's scales
revealing insights from beyond and behind the asteroid.

And so, we shine, brighter than shadows.
Inversions of understandings.
Flip the microscope over,
and peer at the crystalline shine of opposites.
The secret magic of an occultist's mind,
inherited in, and by, whispering disembodied form.
Absorbed eagerly. Voraciously.
Wordless stories, wondrous glories,
non-existent beings, osmotic, fused energies.
Voices are silent when energy moves.

Individual interpretations of witchcraft
are so varied, they are not even the same thing,
like the philosophies of past thinkers.
Heart chakras create
drifting and shifting dawnings in spacetime
while Third Eyes in universal word-rhyme
stare through multi-dimensional boxes.

Father, I know not what I see,
but I do know it is not meant for me.
How real is the steely feel of these abstract revelations?

Open my soul, more than I can.
Show me something that is past mere ideas.

Move through me and deposit a truth.
I know you will refuse,
my unworthiness is so vast,
as invisible yet all-pervasive as the air.
You're barely there.

Yesterdays, distant, distorted, tomorrows,
a tease reminiscent of the Tantalus myth,
empty spaces and doubts, all pith.
Mysteries and speculation of foggy and
unopened doors into voids and nowheres.
I am old, I am tired,
I took the same road at every fork as I
would again, today,
there is underground contentment
without any brush with
an uncertainty principle.
The caves and caverns of my covert choices.

I am wiser, I am closer, I can see the sunset.
The journey was so much longer, and slower,
than I dared imagine,
my teachers were largely anonymous,
or was it all just the one life
and all its experiences
from which the citadel was constructed?
When my road ends,
THE road extends, ever on,
souls joining and leaving when and where they must.

The ashes to the ashes, and the dust to the dust.

Year of the Dragon

There is a scorch, it prevails a life-force in
simultaneous, egregious tone;
under sparkling effervescence and
elephantine bulk, crawling beneath
intermittent, clockwork geyser spurts of
steam and teardrop-petalled blooms.

An eyelid lifts and closes with equal
severity amid milk-white flesh and grey bone;
over bubbling, spurts of mud flat
screamers in the purple-tainted and
orange-tinted hailstone rock. Hideaway
below swampish jumbled rooms.

Reptilian oceanic poison fish puffs along
by sea-snake squeezer, all alone;
trapezium scowler amid the snowflake
torture, and the brown scooter, and the
nightdreamer. A Rat dashes up a drainpipe
swimming into witch-hovered brooms.

Complexity found in confounded
floundered weightless swim bladder cone;
where is the mist? I heard it spooned
briskly by neighbourhood laughter, the
village idiot missed the incoherent haze of
a secret chamber only reached by crooms.

CATACLYSMIC VIBRATIONS

Astabular butream cotlerious derchipp-erenkyladra,
fripchipskipper gornish hone,
istrious jorbin, kerpimil looomieg
motrewbia nisset oppyba pruvish, quaxian
roptipop survasat tinky udfitrob vaspawig
wajx xybollic yeffayiffayooffaa zooms.

In the Year of the Dragon, energies go
through the roof, or believers in the clone;
the Sheep and Snake and Scorpion are a
singular snooper sensibility gatecrashing
invader, while the Year of the Ox is rocks.
A lonely witchy telepinks her toppest brooms.

Underdog undercat pet cemetery excellent
business idea. Don't eat the mascarpone;
underscore necessary in the mystery of
the passwording, choose eighteen
characters and memorise. Never chastise.
Never compromise. Or eat the shrooms.

In the Year of the Cat there's a song, but
you can call me 'Al'. Play the trombone;
play bass, but backwards. Become famous
without knowing why or how,
because the tape was tweaked
by Tiny Tim on a whim. He eats Vim, in pooms.

The pooms and poems have to be pointed out.
The poots and poets can condone;
playing tricks. Poets can invent wourds,
so can anybody.

An edelweiss costs a fucker of a price,
because they're both rare, and nice,
like saffron, the spice. Plooms.

Astrology is made up, yet it's also all true,
like the Year of the Monkey is someone;
the bigwanker is so so so much like a
perverted spanker in a secret location
over a bridge to eternity, across faery tales
into realms where terror weaves looms.

Year of the Rooster,
give the kids a booster, squirt the dirt, a spurt shone;
of yogurt. Spend the night in a yurt.
Ejaculations of inoculations are pure
speculation. Keep your fucking gob shut.
You're in a rut? See if I give a nut's wooms.

Archer, fire. Fish, conspire. Twins, flame.
Lion, mane. Bull, run. Scales, tip one;
Crab, pinch. Scorpion, flinch. Ram, barge.
Goat, charge. Water carrier, carry water,
and don't drop it or you'll cop it. Poison Ivy
is climbing the walling, brides and grooms.

There's so much sublime grime at this
prime time, and much to atone;
loads-a-money up for grabs in the labs,
they're the place to be. You listen to me.
Obadiah, Jeremiah, get back on your
funeral pyre. Before yoo presooms.

Whalesong is really strong even if it lasts

CATACLYSMIC VIBRATIONS

so fucking long, eat up your scone;
smoking a bong can go wrong. It can go
absolutely Pete Tong actually. Actively.
Neural pathways are fast, hold power, up the tower,
each hour, like the flower. Eat up your legooms.

Mr. Uppity, that's me. I live in a tree.
Nobody can reach me. But everyone;
can see me. It's not really me. The Royal We.
I'm a fungus. Humongous. Catch the
fucking bus. You ain't one of us. Blow the
fucking doors off. And fuck off. Kabooms!

There's a sweetness to Caroline, but she
can't join us. She doesn't know Room 101;
or that the password is 'Swordfish'.
The combination to the safe is safe, it's been
memorised, by a Chinese girl with a perfect memory.
She's in empty rooms.

Scaramanga, he of the third tit,
and priceless weapon, has testosterone;
what are noon spanner octahedra wanting
with all that jam? Open up, it's the police!
We have a search warrant. We know you
have the Golden Fleece in your spooms.

Rasputin, the funky monk, and his mountain
of fucking junk, also possesses hormone;
shoot him last week, that's an order. Do it
across the border or he'll be a hoarder of disorder
and go to live in Mordor. Or visit
the barber at the harbour. Boom booms.

CATACLYSMIC VIBRATIONS

Quasimodo, dead as a Dodo, bird of lore,
unable to fly but right in the zone;
creature comforts the sad dinosaurus
and slip into shadows just before they saw us.
Single file towards the Nile. Building pyramids
takes such a long time - aphial wombs.

The moral of this riddiculus hippocampus is as such.
Venture-dentures like art and music and righting
are media for expressssion
and there are no rools to the game.
You could fart at a tart if you thought it was smart
or if you decided it was art.

Feel free to disobay evrything
in order to create anything.
If peeple disagreeee with thee,
it's just not important.

Take time to Be.

The Eyes of Azrael

Something will have to give,
I'm losing the will to live.
I long to see the shade of my blood,
which hue of immaculate red?
I have longed to hear and to feel
the blade of Damascus steel,
whatever the shape formed by fire -
in flesh, there is no pariah.

To drop, by a rope, from a tree?
The romance of that attracts me.
The snap of my neck, like a whip -
do I doubt that wish to let rip?
Yet the question itself shows the fear.
The sprites on my shoulders are here!
The Devil and Angel competing,
for they know suicide can be fleeting.

The Devil begins with his greeting;
"young man, as the peace in your sleeping,
eternally you will be calm
and safe. My words are a charm."

The Angel flies forth in a lightbeam,
then showers Yours Truly with sunstream,
casts images of seraphic wonder,
blasts breezes of zephyrous thunder.

CATACLYSMIC VIBRATIONS

The Universe, watching with care,
steps forward, unstaring her stare.
Ponders with a feminine glare,
her verdict will be royally fair.

"I choose an equality pact.
The cosmos half-white and half-black.
Between you, the Yang and the Yin.
Secrets shared, the Out and the In.
The Sun and the Moon owning Sky.
Ladyhawke, wishing to fly.
The Earth, a blanket of soil,
the Ocean, a carpet of oil.
All balance will never fall down,
but regenerate through light and sound."

My survival is still undecided.
My matter and mind have collided.
My ego and id merge in lithium.
A universal equilibrium.

Fourteenth Frequency Riddle

In the resonance that manifests
Out of thin air and white cloud vacuum
Iceberg's depths, deceptive, dead
Breathless pain. Where is my home?
I am in absence of clue or map
Thunderous beam of cardiac ventricle
Echo, nymph of Kithairon, toys
And plays with soundscape lyres.
Open chord across arc and arch
There's Pi, and Phi, and tantric Chi
Underwells burst ungrateful
Here, there are more answers than questions
There, hear spherical music enchantment
Hedonist orgy of Lord Bacchus
And Pipes of Pan, he of cloven hoof
Octagonal prism over blue flame
Yellow orchid upon altar of quartz
Burrow below miniature cave
Icicle, stalactite scratches molten sun
Osmium density clearing summer's edge
The genie is vapour.
Undress the soul.
Feel vibrating source energy pool
Amid warted lizards cackling smiles
Jellyfish bobbing, bouncing they float
Osprey on the breeze and not the sea.
My calculations are faulty.
Meltdown flows between ogres and trolls
Shadow box

CATACLYSMIC VIBRATIONS

Enlil of Mesopotamia waves to approve
Odin breathes an iron spear
At Temperance, Temperance is calm.
Untrigger for an epoch and for vain hope
Flight and fight, what else can there be?
Implements of torture machinery gleam
The wounds are fatal
Schematics find the extinct animal
And black obelisks of a pillared obsidian bell.
Terrified of turning the blind corner
Serpentine dream and hallucination pit
Swallow those who dare to mock
Fossilised in ancient amber bones
The face of the glass and a clock
Clicking timescapes, stranded
The Eagle Has Landed
But it looks like a starfish.
Learn to count
On a treadmill
Disembody from shape
The party started without you
The abundance, decadence, glee
Untroubled are the vicious dogs
A pagoda, a gazebo in the pretty garden
See the patterns in the numbers
The grand design, the random accidents
Opened portals to dimensionless limbo.
Inhale the burn
Try to exhale the poisonous death
The dread will suffocate, asphyxiate you
Rise through ashen char
Fall with fresh battle scar

CATACLYSMIC VIBRATIONS

Eat the living, wriggling squid
In a tunnel of potato flower
Can you feel the weight of the statue
That pins you to the beachy sand
Incongruous as a hammerhead shark?
Open your eyes.
Gaze into the black heart of Satan
There isn't anything there but a lie, like God.
Your Bible is vacant space
Narrate the story to a girl or boy
And hear the laughter of their wisdom and intuition
A giggle as they see beyond your horizon
Firing an arrow at an angel
And its frivolity. It's frivolity.
The vortex of time in a tree
Ugly, pummelled, disfigured
A cord of umbilica in a permanent knot
Can you see that randomised tale
Of three cities
Sodom, Gomorrah, Babylon
The unknown is known.
A pyramid of perfect
Immaculate design
Will the architects ever return
With the secrets
My guess is they don't care to
And why is the sky?
It's all there in Voynich
But deliberately undecipherable,
By all means try, and try, and try
Until the day you die, knowing nothing,
In mud, madness, obscenity and obscurity

CATACLYSMIC VIBRATIONS

Scream and walk, in shivery circles in your cell
Break your skull against the wall
Crack your cranium against the darkness and the stone
The prison where they incarcerate you
Because they misunderstand and fear you
They cannot stand to be near you
And they cannot explain you
And they don't want to
Any more than you do.
This is a bavarium and a parable
About kaleidoscopes, sculptures and relics
Way-out psychedelics, fly agarics
Food for the fragments of the mind.
Petrified as a forest of fright
Or an entanglement of glacial crawling
A plague of locusts descends
By nature and not high command
To shade the sky with a blackened sheet
Near where spies speak of their ideas
Gallantry, a thing of the past.
Dog-eat-dog, loyalty is out of fashion
It's all about survival and the currency of trust.

Looking over your shoulder every moment.
Integrity is bought and sold like bags of sugar.
After the war
The one between true and false
Not the spoon-fed faeces
There will be nothing left behind
To eat or live in or even look at
Stay in the land of make-believe
With your two living friends

CATACLYSMIC VIBRATIONS

Desert rain spitting into our hair
Desert mudness of sand and splash
Sidewinding snakes
Drought
Feeling the creeping dehydration
Scalding rays
Burning blisters
A night of star and fruit and grime
Carry carrion and skeletal remains
Scattering chattering chipper chop chimes
How to find life? Galactic order?
There is no more of that.
Fly with the bird
No paradise to see
Encased in case of emergency bridge,
Find a way to make the team game.

One

**There are Two sides to every story, including this One.
There is only One side that One can be on, the side of Humanity.
Our blood is of One colour on both sides.**

Vladimir Putin doesn't strike me as a man
whose buttons you should press,
whose boundaries you should test;
at least, that is unless
you're a Dopey Joe,
or a BoJo,
with approval ratings in the sewer
and a heart that's angel-pure.

The peace police, the UN,
with its white-honest, toothless men,
turns a blind eye to the States
when they're marshalling their mates.

'International Law'
is touted as the cure.

The shedding of Ukrainian blood,
the trampling in Ukrainian mud,
a price worth paying, apparently,
it's not our boys, it isn't me.

Vladimir had asked for space,
it wasn't just a loss of face,
but safety from a NATO sprawl.
Insidious, an Eastward crawl,
missiles up the Russians' arse,
a territorial terror clasp;

"Democracy is King!" we scream,
the compulsory American Dream.

Now, Vladimir's no choirboy saint.
A 'cheeky chap' he really ain't.
Everyone's friend If the money's right.
Never one to duck a fight.
I'm not a fan, by any means,
but Uncle Sam has all the 'Greens'.

Cut the Russian money flow!
No need to send in G.I.Joe,
a cleaner scrap, no blood to spill,
a strangling - a nice, soft kill.

"Uncle Sam, whaddya know?"
The latest propaganda show.
Uncle Sam would do the same
if he didn't already own the game.

No One wins

Glasshouses and Stones
Requiem and Resurrection

I

The filter, the film, the fish-eye lens,
the form through the fissure,
so dreadful and dark,
devoid of a spark,
a shapeshifting shadow.

My vantage point is a vapid vortex.
Complicit with my cerebral cortex.
Darker than the darkest of matter.
Shimmering, smashed shards of a shatter.

II

The silhouette is a visible dream
of a terrifying consciousness stream
or the splashing of acid that melts my face
into twists and mists of time or space
into which I fall at terminal velocity
and formulate my fearful philosophy
as I speculate in a lucid lake
where I drown and drift and bend and break
and frown and scowl and grimace and growl
in a vampire's laugh and a werewolf's howl,

I'm in the clasp of a vice's grip
or is it the grasp of a frightened slip

down the hollow shaft of a sacred tomb
to a timeless trance in a redshift room,
I can feel the heat of the scorching beam
as a laser burns through my self-esteem.

III

My eyes. My mind. My sight.
Life shifts to black from white.
Our world, it is controlled,
by beings hot and cold,
they frame our supervision,
through print and television.

To focus all our pain,
unless we can abstain,
resist, react, refrain,
recoil, reject, retain
our dignity and strength
to hold them at arm's length.

IV

Sovereign entities we are.
With every wound and scar,
we grow, and fight, and spar,
and watch, and learn, and wait,
and study, and create,
and form a mental state
that they cannot penetrate
and so may not impregnate.

CATACLYSMIC VIBRATIONS

Cocooned in diamond shells,
we are protected from the spells
and the curses of the dark,
every rattlesnake and shark.

Every message is in code.
A signpost on a road.
They give the game away
with every word they say.

None of it's real, it's a trance,
a gamble, a throw of dice,
trickery and treats,
an infestation of lice.

Step back. Analyse.
See past. Become wise.
Watch the void behind the eyes.
Hear the empty, shallow lies.
Then rise, and rise, and rise.

They'll take you for a ride.
Pick a path. Choose a side.
Eat the shit. Spit it out.
Lose your fear. Lose your doubt.

The blindfold is voluntary,
So remove it.
Pop the cherry.
Pass the sherry.
Be merry.

Methuselah and Sphinx

Liquid time, in the company of strangers,
familial friends, and acquaintances,
pushing through the fence,
without pretence, in the present tense.

Sonic boom, empty-roomers and hydrangeas,
ox-bow bends, open my chest,
despite the torrential bloodspill,
down the hill, beside the paper mill.

Gathered pace, orchestral rearrangers,
it never ends, hoverflies at sunrise,
biting flesh, that tastes so fresh,
and looks like Gilgamesh;
but feels like Odin's rage.

This shadow of a shadow
cannot be detected, or resurrected.
It dwells within its cavern of Satanic void.
A child's nursery, of innocence
and of blackened fright, or frightened night.

Liquid time, drains away,
into the swamps of the day.
From the care and the core
of yesterday's oasis,
in ambiguous colours,
and a flux of active epistasis.

CATACLYSMIC VIBRATIONS

The pungent, the acid, the acrid, the sulphur,
a crack of trachea, bulge of inflamma.
A glacier melting before it can budge,
it turns to sludge. It bears a grudge.

The three Dark Mages,
Abaddon, Beelzebub and Choronzon,
Demons in Echoing Fire,
Gargoyles of Hell,
inside Jezebel's kiln
or a languid mausoleum of nature.
Ocelots prancing, as if
Queens of
raspberry and strawberry trees,
underneath valiant, wolverine xenophobes
in yellow zoos.

And that was the use
of the compass of the N.E.W.S.

The Visibility of the Toxicity

It's the Agenda.
The Propaganda.
Rammed down our throats,
from Land's End to John O'Groats.
The year is Twenty Twenty Two,
the Ownership of Me, and You.
Our Freedom, Eroded,
our Reality, Decoded,
our Nerves, Corroded
by Explosives, Exploded.
The Media Manipulation
and Messaging Mutation,
this Viral Velocity,
this COVID Conspiracy,
controlled Communications,
Cancerous Collaborations,
the Agenda,
the Propaganda.

Orwell foresaw it,
'Nineteen Eighty-Four-d' it,
Huxley foretold it,
like the Walls of Colditz,
Prisons made of Words,
Immunities of Herds,
Diseases that we Breathe
through the Webs our Spiders Weave;
the World Wide Needles jab
like the Pincers of a Crab,

CATACLYSMIC VIBRATIONS

which pierce our feeble skin
to inject their wares within.
Thoughts bent like Metals,
using Vices and Vessels
and Darkness and Light,
by Day and by Night,
each sense is a Courier,
a Deliverer, a Poisoner.

Perpetual Motion
Divides our Devotion.
Devilish Distractions,
Fatal Attractions.
Stimuli Stretched,
like Eternity Etched
on the Minds and the Hearts
and the Maps and the Charts.
Our paths and our view.
Our Compass is True.
Malleable Men,
Masked brethren,
Whispers in Ears
draw Laughter and Tears.
Control is the Aim,
the Psyche the Frame,
the Agenda.
The Propaganda.

Those Grips made of Lies
are Imaginary ties.
Autonomy's Intact
if the Software is hacked.

Retention of belief;
your Soul is your Chief.
As you tuned yourself in,
you may tune out again.
Take hold of your truth,
climb onto the roof,
look around and about,
see the Sky through the doubt.

These Houses of Cards
are in a Typhoon of Rage,
bars made from your Own Will
are forming that Cage.
The Surrender of Power
is an Optional Act;
that's not a Matter of Opinion.
It's a Matter of Fact.

Cataclysmic Vibrations

Earthquake

I think that it might be helpful
to enter the realm of the hypothetical.
I hear the impotent screaming, daily,
of the frustrations and fears
of the people that feel dwarfed by 'The Machine'.

There is the unmistakable deft wrench
of millions of weary tufts of receding hair
being torn from gammon-red scalps,
despite the fact that the Gammon
are the enemy and not the ally.

If I pop off to the World Wide Web,
that used to be a place where -
it was possible to share -
any opinion, or viewpoint,
on that social media that they have on there.

The Facebook or the Twitter
where so many folks are bitter,
but up until a short while ago
we were not subject to a census of censors,
and our voices were not thumped with hammers,
that trumped our creations.

And so, hypothetically,
I wish to paint some little pictures,
and they won't be quaint,
they'll be positively, potentially,
cataclysmic……..but fret not, ye faithful;
they are, also, meaningless, toothless,
without the actual actions required.
Do nothing, and nothing happens,
nothing changes - "nothing to see here,
move along now.
As you were."

Ten years ago, it seems like double,
I analysed my vision,
made a trivial decision,
an experimental excision,
you could say.

I had never been one for newspapers.
Do I honestly need to explain why?
In the desire to avoid miscommunication,
in case there is anyone not keeping up,
I shall elaborate somewhat.
Bear with me awhile.

Wildfire

The word 'propaganda' can confuse,
when it pops up on the news,
because it is very carefully used.
It is not a word that is meant to amuse.
You will never hear it said
about a country you are not supposed
to hate and mistrust.
Just the others.
It describes the use of a technique, or four.
The purpose is to open and close a door
that controls, limits, access, moulding
of information, to and from, your mind.

Repetition, of things, makes you believe them,
regardless of whether they're true.

Omission, of things, keeps you from being aware
of them at all, even if they're true.

Misinformation, that's lies to you and me,
stated, by a smart suit, as if they're facts.

Context, is a tool,
framing the nature of information,
to augment what appears to be true.

For most of my life, all those things
were oddly obvious to me.
Feelings of discomfort, even as a child.

I did not understand it, but I felt it.
In time the mists drifted away,
leaving an open view, of what is truly true.

On those platforms of webs,
the censored words of the plebs,
that vanish mysteriously
as if they had never been there,
like puffs of frosted flowers of air,
invisible but here and there.
We can miss the point of the game,
because it's the physical world, and not the virtual,
that forms the frame.

Television, radio, the printed word;
it's believed if it is seen and heard.
But if it looks like a turd,
feels like a turd,
and smells like a turd,
yeah,
it's a fucking turd.

Hurricane

The media. The 'MSM'.
Trawl that internet thing,
and hear the alarm bells ring.

Turn on the telly at six.
Study the magic tricks.
The repetition, the omission,
the lies, the propaganda,
the twists and tweaks in the context,
the implications.

Daily pandemic briefings,
did you catch the stench on the wind?
Did they scare you,
and make you queue
for a piece of that miracle of science?

Every 'expert' on the BBC
is an employee, of the BBC.
One face can be;
Foreign Affairs correspondent.
Arts correspondent.
European editor.
American editor.
Medical correspondent.
Names always repeated at the front
and the back of the report,
repetition, often effective
but familiarity can breed contempt, too.

CATACLYSMIC VIBRATIONS

I know I'm not surprising you,
with the news about the News,
the North, the East, the West and the South.
If your eyes see what's going on
you need to shut your nosy mouth.

They're just businesses, these news providers and the suits.
Proper voices, nowadays positive discrimination,
token representation of minorities. Not subtle!
The friendly faces, respectable and so professional.

One day, with the accumulation
of the holding back of my urges
to throw a rock at the screen,
I'd had it. Enough was enough.
They were in my house! They're in yours.

Nobody in that rancid pinnacled club
got a penny of mine, from that day.
No TV Licence, you just have to sign a form
and stop watching. Done.
And the newspapers?
Handy as back-up
if there's ever a shortage of toilet rolls.

Tsunami

I have a dream.

Money is their lifeblood, their raison d'être,
disguised, transparently, as a service.
My money and everyone else's money
are the foundation stones of the ivory towers
and glass-walled office sanctuary chambers.

We feel them every day, as they perform their osmosis.
Their oblique mazes ensnaring our open brains.
The sour and the sharp poisons of fragrant citrus;
it makes the heart howl and scowl
but that helpless sensation is another
obtuse, optical trick.

Here it is.
You take the red pill or the blue.
It's completely up to you.
It always has been, Neo.
It always has been.
That small price of your tabloid,
your pocket of media oxygen,
you're allowed to keep it, from them.

It belongs to you.

Those complaints you make to your webnob friends,
the rage, the powerlessness and the hopelessness,
are in the palm of your own crusty, bleeding hand

for you to do with exactly as you wish.
You have no need of my permission,
but I give it to you now, anyway, with love.

I know that you wonder and despair
whether this faceless iron claw
can ever be fought and defeated,
and how it could be done?

I am leading you to water
but I cannot make you drink,
but the good news is
you are a sentient, salient being,
and not a horse or a camel.
The 'revolution' can look like this:
keep your money in your sporran.
Away from the printed media,
and the broadcast media,
from the grasp of your oppressors.
Then see it all collapse, and implode,
silently, peacefully, devastatingly.

Or instead find a reason to prefer,
and defer to,
the status quo.